15 MOST DANGEROUS PLACES ON EARTH

Discovering the Forbidden,
Mysterious, and Deadly Locations
That Challenge Human
Understanding

ERIC R. WACHTER

Copyright © 2025 by Eric R. Wachter

All rights reserved. The content of this publication may not be reproduced, distributed, or transmitted in any form or by any means, including photocopying, recording, or other electronic or mechanical methods, without the prior written permission of the publisher, except for brief quotations incorporated into critical reviews and specific noncommercial uses allowed by copyright law.

Table of Contents

Introduction..3
Chapter 1: The Death Valley Mystery..........................5
Chapter 2: The Gates to Hell..11
Chapter 3: North Sentinel Island.................................15
Chapter 4: The Bermuda Triangle............................... 22
Chapter 5: Mount Everest's Death Zone....................29
Chapter 6: Snake Island..36
Chapter 7: Chernobyl Exclusion Zone.......................42
Chapter 8: Antarctica's Perils.......................................49
Chapter 9: Lake Natron... 56
Chapter 10: The Devil's Sea...63
Chapter 11: Aokigahara Forest....................................69
Chapter 12: The Boiling River of the Amazon..........76
Chapter 13: The Haunted Catacombs of Paris.........82
Chapter 14: Mariana Trench...89
Chapter 15: The World's Loneliest Place.................. 95
Conclusion.. 102

Introduction

The world is full of places where few dare to tread, hidden corners of the earth that seem to pulse with an energy both unnerving and irresistible. These are destinations that evoke a sense of awe and terror in equal measure—places where danger lurks behind every shadow and mystery hangs in the air like a thick fog. From remote islands to abandoned towns, from treacherous mountains to depths of the sea, there exist locations that hold the power to ignite both fear and fascination. But what is it about these places that makes them so perilous, so untouchable, and yet, so undeniably alluring?

Some of these places have a history steeped in the blood of those who've dared to enter, their stories echoing through time as chilling reminders of nature's power and humanity's fragility. Others are shrouded in the unknown, the questions surrounding them so deep and unsettling that the very thought of uncovering their secrets sends a shiver down the spine. These places seem to call to us, drawing us in with their dangerous allure. But only the bravest—or most foolish—have ever tried to venture into their depths.

This book takes you on a journey to explore the *15 most dangerous places on Earth*, each one more intriguing and mysterious than the last. You will uncover the untold stories that have shaped these locations, from ancient legends to the modern-day tales of those who've attempted to conquer them. What makes them so dangerous? What secrets are they hiding? And why do humans dare not enter these forbidden places?

As we step into the unknown, prepare yourself for a journey that will keep you on the edge of your seat. With every page, the stories of these dangerous destinations will reveal themselves, and you'll find yourself wondering—how much would you risk to uncover the truths hidden in the world's most mysterious and perilous places? Keep reading, and brace yourself for a tale that will leave you with more questions than answers, but a deep, unshakeable curiosity that you won't be able to ignore. The journey begins now.

Chapter 1: The Death Valley Mystery

Death Valley, located in the eastern part of California's Mojave Desert, is one of the most extreme and unforgiving places on Earth. It is a land where the sun blazes relentlessly, and the temperature can soar to unimaginable heights. It holds the title of the hottest place on Earth, with temperatures regularly exceeding 120°F (49°C) during the summer months. But the harsh climate is only part of what makes Death Valley a place of mystery.

Beyond the parched sands and scorching heat, the valley is home to a series of enigmatic phenomena that have baffled scientists and explorers alike for centuries. Among the most perplexing of these are the famous "sailing stones," large boulders that appear to move on their own across the desert floor, leaving long, visible trails behind them. These stones, which can weigh hundreds of pounds, have sparked theories ranging from the scientific to the supernatural, captivating the imagination of all who hear their strange tale.

The sailing stones are perhaps one of Death Valley's most famous mysteries. They are found scattered across the Racetrack Playa, a dry lakebed located in the northern part of the valley. For decades, explorers and scientists have been drawn to the site to witness the phenomenon firsthand, but for years, the true cause of the stones' movement remained elusive. The rocks, some of which are as large as a small car, leave behind long, winding tracks in the cracked, dried earth, some of which extend hundreds of feet.

What is most baffling is that these stones appear to move without any human intervention, animal activity, or any other obvious cause. At first glance, it seems as though they might be rolling or sliding across the surface of the playa, but how could such heavy stones move on their own, without any force being applied to them?

The mystery of the sailing stones was compounded by the fact that no one ever actually witnessed the stones in motion. They would appear one day, having moved across the desert floor, leaving behind tracks that could not have been caused by wind or any other obvious natural force. These tracks often seemed to form an intricate pattern, as though the stones were making deliberate, purposeful movements.

Over the years, many theories arose attempting to explain the phenomenon. Some claimed that the rocks were moved by ancient spirits or supernatural forces, while others suggested that the stones could be rolling in the dead of night when no one was watching, pushed by an unseen force. But none of these explanations could be proven, leaving the mystery unresolved for many years.

In the early 2000s, scientists finally began to unravel the mystery of the sailing stones, but not without considerable effort and a great deal of time. It wasn't until 2014 that a group of researchers, equipped with GPS devices and time-lapse cameras, were able to capture the stones in motion. After years of speculation, the scientists discovered that the movement of the rocks was a natural phenomenon caused by a combination of weather conditions. The rocks didn't move on their own, but rather, they were pushed by a rare and unusual event.

During the winter months, Death Valley can experience occasional rainstorms, which are usually followed by freezing temperatures at night. When the conditions are just right, a thin layer of ice forms on the surface of the Racetrack Playa, creating a slick, slippery surface. The wind then pushes the ice sheet, and the stones become trapped within it. As the ice begins to melt, the stones slide slowly across the playa, leaving behind the distinctive trails that have fascinated scientists for so long. The movement is so gradual and slow that it was impossible to observe with the naked eye, but through the use of technology, the scientists were able to confirm that this was the explanation behind the sailing stones.

This discovery didn't diminish the mystery, though. It only added another layer of intrigue to the story. While scientists had finally unraveled the mystery behind the stones' movement, the rare combination of factors required to make the rocks move meant that the phenomenon was still a fascinating and elusive spectacle. The precise timing of the weather conditions and the necessary amount of ice and wind made it an event that only occurred once every few years, if at all. And even though the mystery was solved, the haunting question of why the rocks leave such elaborate, seemingly intentional tracks behind them still lingers in the minds of those who study them.

The sailing stones are not the only challenges faced by explorers and scientists who venture into Death Valley. The valley itself is a harsh and inhospitable environment, making it a dangerous place for anyone who dares to explore its vast and empty expanse. The extreme heat, which can exceed 130°F (54°C) during the hottest months, poses a significant risk of heatstroke and dehydration. Water sources are scarce, and navigating the terrain can be difficult, even for experienced adventurers. The valley's remote location, far from civilization, only adds to the challenge. Death Valley is also prone to sudden and intense sandstorms that can reduce visibility to near zero, making it easy to become disoriented and lost.

Despite these risks, Death Valley continues to attract scientists, photographers, and adventurers. Its harsh beauty and mysterious phenomena, like the sailing stones, draw people who are eager to solve its riddles and uncover its secrets. For those who are willing to brave the scorching heat and the dangers of the desert, the rewards are considerable. The valley offers a rare opportunity to witness nature's most extreme forces at work, and to be part of the ongoing exploration of one of Earth's most unique landscapes.

While the sailing stones may have been explained by science, there are still many other mysteries that linger in the vastness of Death Valley. From ancient petroglyphs etched into rock faces to unexplained lights in the sky, the valley holds many secrets yet to be uncovered. For those with the courage and curiosity to explore this extraordinary place, Death Valley remains a land of both danger and discovery—a place where the line between science and myth is blurred, and where the unknown continues to beckon.

Chapter 2: The Gates to Hell

In the heart of Turkmenistan, nestled within the vast expanse of the Karakum Desert, lies a place that has earned the chilling nickname "The Gates to Hell." The Darvaza Gas Crater, a gaping hole in the earth that has been burning for decades, is a natural wonder that defies logic and stirs the imagination. It is a site that simultaneously fascinates and terrifies, drawing adventurers, scientists, and curious souls from across the globe who are all eager to witness firsthand the spectacle of an eternal fire that refuses to be extinguished.

The crater itself, roughly 230 feet in diameter and 98 feet deep, was created by a gas explosion that occurred in 1971 when Soviet scientists were drilling for natural gas. The ground beneath the drilling rig collapsed, forming a massive crater that exposed pockets of natural gas deep within the earth. In an attempt to prevent the spread of methane gas, which is highly toxic and explosive, the scientists decided to set the crater alight, hoping the fire would burn off the gas over time. What was meant to be a temporary measure turned into a lasting inferno, one that has been burning continuously ever since. Today, the Darvaza Gas Crater stands as an unyielding symbol of both human error and nature's raw power, an eternal flame that burns against the backdrop of the desert's stark, unforgiving landscape.

Local legends and myths surrounding the Darvaza Crater paint it as a place of great mystery and danger. For centuries before the drilling incident, the area was known to the Turkmen people as a cursed land. The desert was filled with stories of hidden treasures, lost caravans, and strange phenomena. Some local tribes believed that the land was home to powerful spirits, and the flames from the crater were seen as a manifestation of these spirits' wrath. They thought that the crater was a portal to the underworld, a gateway through which the spirits of the dead could pass into the afterlife, and it became a place of reverence and fear. Travelers were warned not to venture too close, as it was said that the flames would consume anyone who dared to approach.

Over time, these stories became ingrained in the local culture, further mystifying the crater and adding to its eerie reputation. Some believed that the flames held the power to heal or curse, depending on how they were approached, while others told of strange occurrences around the crater—unexplained sounds in the night, sudden shifts in the air, or bizarre visions witnessed by those who camped near the fire. As a result, the Darvaza Gas Crater became not just a natural wonder, but a symbol of the unknown, a place where science and myth collided in a way that few could explain.

From a scientific perspective, the Darvaza Gas Crater plays a significant role in understanding the complex natural processes that shape our planet. The crater is part of a vast underground network of natural gas reserves, and the fire that has been burning for over fifty years is essentially a giant flare designed to release and burn off the methane gas that has accumulated beneath the surface. The intense heat and light from the flames are a testament to the sheer power of the earth's natural gas reserves. While many might see the burning crater as a failure of human intervention, it has nonetheless contributed to the study of geology and environmental science. The continuous fire serves as a reminder of the volatile and unpredictable nature of the Earth's crust.

In terms of its environmental impact, the Darvaza Gas Crater has raised concerns about the potential consequences of releasing such large quantities of methane—a potent greenhouse gas—into the atmosphere. Despite the burning fire's seemingly spectacular display, experts have noted that methane emissions from the site contribute to climate change. The burning gas does, in fact, limit the immediate environmental risk by preventing the uncontrolled release of methane, but it also adds to the global carbon footprint. The ongoing fire at Darvaza remains a paradox—an environmental hazard that simultaneously serves as a cautionary tale about humanity's ability to manipulate nature.

The Darvaza Gas Crater is an enduring testament to the power of both natural forces and human intervention. It stands as a symbol of the unintended consequences that can arise from our quest to extract and exploit the Earth's resources, but it also offers a glimpse into the mysterious, uncharted territories of the world. Whether viewed as a scientific anomaly, a natural wonder, or a mythical gateway to another world, the Darvaza Gas Crater continues to fascinate all who encounter it. Its eternal flames, burning day and night, will likely persist for decades, keeping the mystery of the "Gates to Hell" alive for generations to come.

Chapter 3: North Sentinel Island

North Sentinel Island, located in the Bay of Bengal, stands as one of the last truly isolated places on Earth. This small, remote island is home to the Sentinelese, an indigenous tribe that has remained almost completely untouched by modern civilization for thousands of years. The island, which spans only about 23 square miles, is surrounded by treacherous reefs and is part of the Andaman and Nicobar Islands group, which is controlled by India.

North Sentinel is off-limits to outsiders, and the Indian government has placed strict laws prohibiting anyone from approaching the island. Despite these legal barriers, North Sentinel has captured the fascination of explorers, anthropologists, and adventurers for decades, all drawn by the allure of one of the most enigmatic and untamed societies in the world.

The Sentinelese are known for their fierce protection of their territory and their hostility towards outsiders. They have maintained their independence and way of life by remaining in complete isolation from the outside world. No one knows the exact size of the tribe, as they are rarely seen, but estimates suggest that there are anywhere from 50 to 400 members. The tribe has lived on North Sentinel Island for thousands of years, maintaining a hunter-gatherer lifestyle that has remained largely unchanged despite the advancement of global civilization. The Sentinelese are known to use spears, bows, and arrows to hunt and protect their island from intruders, and they have been described as having little to no interest in interacting with people from the outside world.

The island itself is covered in dense tropical forest, with a coastline that is heavily lined with coral reefs. The terrain is rugged, and the water surrounding the island is difficult to navigate, making it an almost impenetrable fortress. The island's isolation has helped preserve the tribe's traditional way of life, and they have remained largely unaware of the outside world. The Sentinelese speak a language that is unknown to outsiders, and their social structure and cultural practices are shrouded in mystery. The tribe has no written history, and little is known about their origins, as they have never left the island to record their story.

For centuries, the island was left largely undisturbed, with occasional sightings of the tribe from passing ships or explorers. However, as the modern world expanded, attempts were made to make contact with the Sentinelese. Early accounts of contact date back to the 19th century when British colonial officers first reported sightings of the tribe. The early explorers were struck by the Sentinelese's apparent hostility towards outsiders, often reacting with aggression when they were approached. These initial encounters led to limited interactions with the tribe, but they were brief and often violent. The British government attempted to establish peaceful relations with the Sentinelese, but these efforts were unsuccessful, and the tribe remained resolute in their rejection of outside contact.

In the 20th century, the Indian government took control of the Andaman and Nicobar Islands and began to monitor the activities of the Sentinelese. The government initially made attempts to contact the tribe through peaceful means, sending anthropologists and missionaries to the island in an effort to establish communication and learn more about the tribe's way of life. These efforts were met with hostility, with the Sentinelese reacting aggressively to the presence of outsiders. On more than one occasion, those who ventured too close to the island were met with a barrage of arrows and other projectiles, forcing them to retreat. The government, recognizing the tribe's desire for isolation, soon adopted a policy of non-intervention, declaring North Sentinel Island a protected area and establishing a no-contact zone around it.

Despite the Indian government's policy, there have been several notable and tragic attempts to make contact with the Sentinelese, with devastating consequences. One of the most famous incidents occurred in 2006 when two fishermen, who had been illegally fishing near the island, were killed by the tribe. The fishermen's boat had drifted too close to the shore, and the Sentinelese, who had never been in contact with the men, attacked them with their arrows, killing them instantly. This tragic event prompted the Indian government to reinforce its no-contact policy, declaring that any further attempts to approach the island would be met with force. The incident also brought international attention to the tribe's extreme isolation and their determination to remain unconnected from the modern world.

In 2018, another tragic and high-profile event occurred when an American missionary named John Allen Chau attempted to make contact with the Sentinelese. Chau, who was a self-proclaimed evangelical Christian, had long been fascinated by the tribe and believed that it was his mission to spread Christianity to them. Despite the warnings from the Indian authorities and the tribe's well-documented hostility towards outsiders, Chau made several attempts to land on the island, eventually succeeding with the help of local fishermen.

Once on the island, he attempted to preach to the tribe, but his efforts were met with immediate hostility. The Sentinelese chased him away with their arrows, and within a day, Chau was dead. His death sparked a fierce debate over the ethics of attempting to make contact with isolated tribes and whether outsiders had the right to interfere with their way of life. The Indian government responded by reinforcing its no-contact policy, and the fishermen who had assisted Chau were arrested and charged for their involvement.

The history of North Sentinel Island is one of isolation and protection. The Indian government has made it clear that the island is off-limits to outsiders, and the tribe's desire to remain untouched by the outside world is respected by most. While the Sentinelese are seen by many as a symbol of humanity's past, their violent rejection of contact with the outside world has led to debates about the ethics of contact with isolated tribes.

Some argue that it is essential to respect their autonomy and allow them to continue living as they have for millennia. Others believe that the Sentinelese should be given access to modern medicine, education, and other resources that could improve their quality of life. However, the tribe's consistent refusal to interact with outsiders has made it clear that they want to remain undisturbed, and efforts to make contact with them have often ended in tragedy.

North Sentinel Island's isolation is what has allowed the Sentinelese to maintain their culture and way of life. The island's geography—remote, difficult to access, and surrounded by dangerous reefs—has kept it a place that few can approach, making it one of the most dangerous and mysterious places on Earth. The tribe's fierce defense of their territory has led to their portrayal as violent and hostile, but to them, it is a matter of survival.

For thousands of years, they have lived free from the influence of the outside world, and their isolation is a powerful reminder of the resilience of human cultures and the deep desire to protect one's way of life. For now, North Sentinel Island remains a forbidden frontier, a place where the modern world has no place and where the Sentinelese continue to live as they always have, untouched by time.

Chapter 4: The Bermuda Triangle

The Bermuda Triangle, also known as the "Devil's Triangle," is one of the most infamous and enigmatic regions on Earth, stretching between Miami, Bermuda, and Puerto Rico. For centuries, this vast area of the Atlantic Ocean has been the site of mysterious disappearances of ships, planes, and their crews, sparking a wide range of theories about what might be causing these strange occurrences. The Bermuda Triangle has captured the imagination of countless people, becoming a subject of legend, speculation, and fear. Some believe it is a region cursed by supernatural forces, while others argue that scientific explanations may hold the key to unlocking its many secrets.

The first known report of mysterious disappearances in the Bermuda Triangle occurred in 1918 when the USS Cyclops, a massive naval vessel carrying over 300 men, disappeared without a trace while traveling from the West Indies to Baltimore. Despite an extensive search, no wreckage or survivors were ever found, and the incident remains one of the most baffling disappearances in the region's history. This event set the stage for the many disappearances that would follow, each adding to the mythos of the Bermuda Triangle and cementing its reputation as a perilous place where ships and planes vanish into thin air.

One of the most notable and widely known disappearances in the Bermuda Triangle occurred in December 1945, when five US Navy bombers, known as Flight 19, disappeared during a routine training mission. The planes, along with their 14 crew members, left Fort Lauderdale, Florida, on a training exercise but were never seen again. The pilots of the planes reported confusion about their location, with some believing they were over the Florida Keys, while others thought they were much farther out to sea.

Radio transmissions from the planes indicated that they were low on fuel and in distress, but the search that followed turned up no wreckage or bodies, further adding to the mystery. To make the story even more perplexing, a rescue plane sent to search for Flight 19 also vanished without a trace, leading to even greater speculation about the Bermuda Triangle's mysterious powers. This event became one of the most famous disappearances associated with the region and drew widespread attention to the ongoing enigma of the Triangle.

Beyond Flight 19, there have been countless other incidents involving ships, planes, and even entire fleets that have disappeared in the Bermuda Triangle over the years. Among these is the case of the "Mary Celeste," a merchant ship found abandoned in 1872, with its cargo intact and no sign of struggle or foul play. The ship's crew was never found, and the cause of the disappearance remains unknown to this day. Another example is the disappearance of the "Witchcraft," a luxury yacht that vanished in 1967 while just a few miles off the coast of Miami.

The yacht's captain, along with a passenger, sent a distress call to the Coast Guard, claiming that they had struck something submerged in the water. However, when the Coast Guard arrived on the scene, they found no trace of the yacht, and the two men were never seen again.

The mysterious nature of these disappearances has fueled numerous theories about what might be causing them. Over time, several scientific explanations have been proposed, some of which attempt to address the unique environmental and geographical conditions of the Bermuda Triangle. One popular theory centers on the presence of large underwater methane gas deposits.

According to this hypothesis, methane gas trapped on the ocean floor can occasionally be released in large bursts, creating a sudden drop in water density. This, in turn, could cause ships to sink almost instantaneously, as the gas would disrupt the water's buoyancy and make it impossible for vessels to stay afloat. While there is evidence that methane gas exists in the region, no conclusive proof has been found that it is responsible for the disappearances in the Bermuda Triangle.

Another scientific theory suggests that the Bermuda Triangle's magnetic fields may be the cause of the mysterious disappearances. The region is known for having unusual magnetic anomalies, which could potentially interfere with the navigation systems of ships and aircraft. This could cause pilots and sailors to lose their bearings and become disoriented, leading them off course and into dangerous situations. Some researchers believe that these magnetic anomalies could explain the frequent reports of compasses malfunctioning and navigational systems going haywire in the

Bermuda Triangle, causing ships and planes to veer off track and eventually disappear.

One theory that has gained traction over the years is the idea that the Bermuda Triangle is the site of a "vortex" or "portal," a phenomenon that causes vessels and aircraft to be sucked into another dimension or time period. This idea suggests that the Bermuda Triangle is a place where the laws of physics are disrupted, allowing for the possibility of time travel, parallel universes, or even extraterrestrial activity. Proponents of this theory argue that the Bermuda Triangle could be a location where reality itself becomes unstable, leading to bizarre and unexplained events. While there is no scientific evidence to support this theory, it remains a popular topic among conspiracy theorists and enthusiasts of the paranormal.

Despite the scientific explanations, the Bermuda Triangle remains a source of mystery and intrigue for many. The unexplained disappearances of ships, planes, and people continue to defy conventional explanation, and the region has become a symbol of the unknown, a place where the boundaries of reality seem to blur. The stories of ships and planes lost forever in the Bermuda Triangle have become part of the folklore surrounding the area, adding to the mystique of the region and further fueling its reputation as one of the most dangerous and mysterious places on Earth.

There is also an emotional and psychological aspect to the Bermuda Triangle's allure. The sense of uncertainty, fear, and wonder that accompanies tales of disappearing vessels and planes has captivated the human imagination for generations. The thought that something so mysterious and potentially dangerous could exist just off the coast of the United States creates an eerie sense of unease, reminding us of the vast and often unpredictable forces of nature that can easily overwhelm us. The Bermuda Triangle serves as a reminder of our vulnerability in the face of the unknown and the vast, unexplored mysteries that lie just beneath the surface of our everyday world.

As the years go by, the Bermuda Triangle continues to intrigue and fascinate, with new theories, stories, and disappearances adding to its already rich history. Whether caused by natural forces, human error, or something far more extraordinary, the Bermuda Triangle remains one of the most dangerous and mysterious places on Earth.

Its ability to challenge our understanding of the natural world, while igniting our curiosity about what lies beyond our grasp, ensures that it will continue to be a subject of debate and speculation for generations to come. As long as the Bermuda Triangle remains shrouded in mystery, it will continue to captivate those who dare to question what might be hidden in its depths.

Chapter 5: Mount Everest's Death Zone

Mount Everest, standing at an imposing 29,032 feet (8,849 meters) above sea level, is the highest point on Earth. For climbers, reaching the summit of Everest is the ultimate achievement, a pinnacle of human endurance and determination. Yet, despite the allure of standing atop the world, Everest is not a place for the faint of heart. The mountain has claimed over 300 lives since people first began summiting it, and it continues to be one of the most perilous challenges in the world. The journey to the summit is fraught with danger, especially within the "death zone," the area above 26,000 feet (8,000 meters), where the air is thin, and climbers face extreme physical and psychological challenges.

As climbers ascend Mount Everest, they must contend with a number of lethal factors, and the higher they climb, the more unforgiving the environment becomes. The death zone is the area above 26,000 feet, where the human body begins to deteriorate due to the extreme altitude. At this height, the oxygen levels in the atmosphere are only one-third of what they are at sea level, making it nearly impossible to breathe without supplemental oxygen. Even the most experienced climbers, equipped with the best gear and acclimatization strategies, can struggle to stay conscious and functioning in these harsh conditions.

The effects of altitude sickness become more pronounced as climbers reach the death zone. The lack of oxygen puts immense stress on the body, and climbers often experience dizziness, confusion, and shortness of breath. Their bodies are no longer able to perform at optimal levels, and their muscles and organs begin to fail. The human brain is especially vulnerable to the effects of low oxygen levels, and climbers may experience hallucinations, impaired judgment, and a distorted sense of time and distance. It's not uncommon for those in the death zone to make poor decisions, such as continuing their ascent past their physical limits or becoming disoriented and unable to navigate their way back down the mountain.

In addition to the physical toll, climbers face the mental challenge of pushing their bodies to the limit while dealing with the overwhelming sense of isolation and extreme cold. Everest's weather conditions are notoriously unpredictable, and storms can strike with little warning. Temperatures in the death zone can plummet to -40°F (-40°C), making it nearly impossible to stay warm even in the most advanced gear. Hypothermia, frostbite, and exhaustion set in quickly, and the longer a climber spends in the death zone, the less likely they are to survive.

For many, the climb to the summit is the culmination of years of training, preparation, and sacrifice. Yet, once they reach the top, they must still make the dangerous descent back down. Statistically, it is not the ascent to Everest that causes most deaths; it is the descent. Many climbers, exhausted from their exertions, become complacent or miscalculate their ability to safely descend. The body's limited oxygen supply, combined with mental fatigue and deteriorating physical conditions, can lead to poor decision-making. Some climbers choose to continue upwards past the time they had planned, hoping to reach the summit despite worsening conditions, only to run out of energy on the descent.

One of the most tragic aspects of Mount Everest is the large number of climbers who die and are left behind on the mountain, particularly in the death zone. The frozen bodies of those who perished while climbing Everest are often left in place, sometimes becoming grim landmarks for other climbers. Over the years, many bodies have become fixtures on the route to the summit, eerily preserved by the extreme cold. One of the most famous bodies on Everest is that of "Green Boots," a climber who died in 1996. His body, clad in green boots and lying just off the main route, serves as a haunting reminder of the mountain's unforgiving nature.

The sheer number of bodies scattered across the slopes of Everest is a testament to the mountain's mercilessness. In many cases, climbers who perish are not immediately recovered due to the risks and complexities involved in retrieving bodies from such extreme altitudes. The high cost of retrieval operations, combined with the dangers posed by Everest's steep and treacherous terrain, often results in climbers being left to their final resting place. Some bodies are eventually brought down by climbers who choose to carry them, but many remain frozen in place, unable to be moved.

The stories of climbers who have died on Everest are as varied as they are tragic. One of the most notorious incidents occurred in 1996, when a fierce storm struck during a group ascent led by famed mountaineer Rob Hall. The storm trapped climbers at high altitudes, and several members of the group were forced to turn back before reaching the summit. Despite the dangerous conditions, Hall and his clients attempted to summit, only to be caught in a deadly blizzard.

Many of those climbers perished on the mountain, including Hall himself. The disaster was later chronicled in the bestselling book *Into Thin Air* by Jon Krakauer, which revealed the harrowing circumstances surrounding the 1996 tragedy. The story of this disastrous expedition underscored the risks of Everest, where poor judgment and uncontrollable circumstances can quickly lead to death.

Another famous death occurred in 2006 when David Sharp, a British climber, died in the death zone after being left behind by fellow climbers who continued their ascent. Sharp was found by another group of climbers, but he had been unable to receive help in time due to the overwhelming nature of the conditions. The sight of his body—alone and frozen on the mountain—provoked intense debate about climbers' ethics in the death zone. Should climbers prioritize their safety above all else, even if it means leaving behind those who are in distress? Or is there a moral obligation to help fellow climbers, even if it endangers one's own life?

Despite the tragic deaths and dangers that accompany the pursuit of Everest's summit, the mountain continues to draw adventurers from around the world. With the allure of being the first to conquer the world's highest peak, or the desire to prove personal strength and endurance, thousands attempt to summit Everest every year. However, the increasing number of climbers has raised concerns about overcrowding, especially during the brief window in May when conditions are most favorable. The sheer number of climbers attempting to summit at the same time creates dangerous bottlenecks, with climbers waiting for hours in the death zone to reach the summit, exposing them to prolonged periods of low oxygen and the deadly consequences of exhaustion.

Mount Everest has become a destination for both seasoned mountaineers and those with less experience who hope to achieve their dream of standing on top of the world. However, the realities of climbing in the death zone are not always understood by those attempting the summit. While the view from the top may be breathtaking, the risks and sacrifices involved in reaching it are far more daunting than most can comprehend. As Everest becomes more accessible to climbers with less experience and fewer resources, the mountain's deadly reputation continues to grow, along with the tragic stories of those who attempted to conquer it but never made it back.

For those who make it to the summit, the victory is often bittersweet. The joy of standing on top of the world is tempered by the awareness of how close they came to death, and the immense toll the mountain exacted on their bodies and minds. And for those who don't make it, the haunting presence of Everest's death zone serves as a reminder of the relentless power of nature, and the unyielding demand it places on those who dare to challenge it.

Chapter 6: Snake Island

Ilha da Queimada Grande, more famously known as Snake Island, is a place that conjures images of isolation, danger, and mystery. Located just off the coast of Brazil, this small island, spanning only about 43 hectares, is regarded as one of the most perilous and forbidden places on Earth. Situated approximately 90 miles (145 kilometers) from São Paulo, Ilha da Queimada Grande has earned its sinister reputation not just because of its remote location, but also because it is home to one of the deadliest creatures on the planet—the golden lancehead pit viper (*Bothrops insularis*).

The island is completely off-limits to the public, and for good reason. The golden lancehead is found nowhere else in the world, making the island a biological hotspot for this species of snake. Its venom is not only potent but incredibly lethal, capable of causing rapid tissue necrosis and death if not treated immediately. While the snake's venom isn't necessarily the most potent in terms of sheer toxicity, its effect on the human body is devastating. The golden lancehead venom causes significant blood clotting and massive tissue damage, which can result in death within hours if not treated with the right antivenom.

The snake's behavior and venom are a testament to the isolated nature of the island. Over thousands of years of isolation, the golden lancehead evolved on Ilha da Queimada Grande into a highly specialized predator. Unlike other snakes that hunt primarily on land, these vipers have adapted to hunt migratory birds that rest on the island during their travels. They are able to strike with incredible accuracy and speed, making them one of the most efficient predators in the animal kingdom. The venom they produce is an evolutionary response to immobilize their prey, allowing them to consume it at their leisure.

On the island, the snakes are the undisputed rulers, and the few creatures that do inhabit the island have adapted to live in harmony with these dangerous inhabitants. Researchers have found that some species of birds and rodents have developed mechanisms to evade the snakes' deadly strikes. Even the trees on the island seem to have evolved to accommodate the presence of the vipers, with their branches growing in ways that limit the snakes' mobility.

The history of Snake Island is as fascinating as its dangerous inhabitants. There is little documentation of when the golden lancehead pit viper first arrived on the island, but it is believed that it was separated from the mainland around 11,000 years ago when rising sea levels cut off the connection between the island and the Brazilian coast. Since then, the snakes have flourished in this isolated environment, becoming a unique species with physical and behavioral traits that are adapted specifically to life on Ilha da Queimada Grande.

While the snakes are the star attraction of the island, their presence has led to a complete ban on human access. The Brazilian government strictly prohibits anyone from visiting Snake Island without a special permit, and even these permits are only granted to scientific researchers who need to study the island's biodiversity. The risk of human fatalities is simply too high, and it's not uncommon for the snakes to attack when they feel threatened or when they come into contact with an intruder. The sheer density of snakes on the island makes it nearly impossible for anyone to traverse the land without encountering them.

The legend of the island's dangers has persisted over the years, and the myths surrounding it only add to the mystery.

One of the more well-known stories is that the island's snakes were put there intentionally by pirates to guard their treasure. The theory suggests that pirates, seeking to protect their hidden riches, introduced the snakes as a natural deterrent to anyone trying to find their hoard. However, there is no concrete evidence to support this tale, and it's more likely that the snakes arrived on the island through natural processes long before the pirate era. Still, the lore surrounding the island continues to capture the imagination of those who hear it.

For centuries, Ilha da Queimada Grande was largely ignored by the outside world, its dangerous reputation keeping most people at bay. However, with advances in technology and an increasing curiosity about remote locations, the island began to attract attention in the 20th century. Still, the Brazilian government remained steadfast in its decision to keep it off-limits to all but authorized personnel. In recent years, several attempts by explorers and tourists to illegally visit the island have been thwarted, and the government continues to enforce the ban vigorously.

The island's isolation has made it a perfect natural laboratory for studying evolution and the effects of long-term geographic isolation on species. Scientists who have been granted access to the island have studied the snakes extensively, trying to understand how they have evolved in such a unique environment. The golden lancehead has become a symbol of the extreme conditions that can arise in isolated ecosystems, where species evolve to survive in ways that would seem impossible elsewhere.

Despite its eerie reputation and the obvious dangers it poses, Snake Island holds a certain allure for those fascinated by the natural world and the power of evolution. The island's dangerous creatures, its history, and the fact that it remains one of the few places on Earth where humans are strictly forbidden to tread, all contribute to its mystique. Ilha da Queimada Grande is a reminder of the raw, untamed power of nature, and how isolation can breed some of the most extraordinary and deadly creatures on the planet.

While the golden lancehead pit viper is undoubtedly the star of the island, its presence serves as a warning about the fragility of ecosystems and the delicate balance of nature. The island is a living testament to the forces of evolution, where isolation has forged a species perfectly adapted to its environment, yet also one of the most dangerous creatures known to man. The fact that Ilha da Queimada Grande is off-limits to all but the most daring researchers serves as a reminder that some places are too dangerous, too mysterious, and too powerful for human exploration. It is a place that will remain locked in the annals of the natural world, where only the bravest and most careful dare to study it from afar.

Chapter 7: Chernobyl Exclusion Zone

The Chernobyl Exclusion Zone, located in northern Ukraine, is a place shrouded in tragedy, haunting memories, and a profound sense of desolation. The events that unfolded in the early morning hours of April 26, 1986, forever altered the landscape, both physically and psychologically. The catastrophic nuclear disaster at the Chernobyl Nuclear Power Plant continues to echo through history, leaving behind not only an environmental disaster but also a deeply ingrained fear and fascination that draws people to the area, especially with the rise of "dark tourism."

The Chernobyl disaster, one of the worst nuclear accidents in history, began as a simple safety test that spiraled disastrously out of control. At 1:23 AM, Reactor No. 4 of the Chernobyl Nuclear Power Plant, located near the town of Pripyat, exploded. The explosion released a massive amount of radioactive particles into the atmosphere, sending deadly radiation over vast areas of Europe. The immediate aftermath was horrific: workers at the plant were killed in the explosion, and those who survived were exposed to dangerous levels of radiation. The fire that followed burned for days, releasing even more radioactive materials into the environment.

In the wake of the explosion, a massive evacuation operation was launched to relocate the people living in the surrounding areas. The city of Pripyat, once home to nearly 50,000 people, was the closest to the plant and the first to be evacuated. Residents were told they would be returning soon, but they never did. Within 36 hours, the entire population of Pripyat was displaced, leaving behind homes, schools, shops, and the remnants of daily life. The eerie emptiness of the town, abandoned so quickly, makes it one of the most haunting and iconic locations in the Exclusion Zone.

The scale of the disaster was vast, but the immediate human toll was just the beginning of the long-term consequences. In the years following the explosion, thousands of people, including emergency workers, soldiers, and plant workers, died from radiation exposure. Many others developed cancers and other radiation-induced illnesses. Entire generations were affected, not only by direct exposure to radiation but also by the psychological trauma of living in the shadow of such an unprecedented disaster. The effects of Chernobyl are still being felt today, with the area around the power plant remaining uninhabitable due to the lingering radiation.

The Exclusion Zone, a 30-kilometer radius surrounding the Chernobyl site, was established to limit human exposure to radiation. It remains largely uninhabited, with only a handful of individuals allowed to enter for scientific research or other approved purposes. The site itself is an environmental wasteland, with forests, rivers, and wildlife slowly reclaiming the land that was once home to thousands of people.

However, the area is not devoid of life. In recent years, wildlife such as wolves, wild boars, and even bison have been spotted in the zone, thriving in an area that remains toxic for humans. Nature, in a way, has begun to heal, but it does so in an eerie, post-apocalyptic setting where humanity's legacy is unmistakably marked by radiation and ruin.

Pripyat, the most notable of the abandoned towns, stands frozen in time. The once-thriving city, built to accommodate the workers of the Chernobyl plant and their families, now lies in ruins. Ferris wheels rust in place, the eerie silence broken only by the howling of the wind through abandoned buildings. Children's toys remain scattered in the dusty rooms of a kindergarten, while gas masks and other remnants of daily life lay untouched. The once-vibrant city, with its schools, amusement parks, and lively streets, is now a ghost town, a grim reminder of what was lost in the wake of the disaster.

The haunting nature of the Chernobyl Exclusion Zone has become a significant draw for tourists, particularly those interested in "dark tourism"—the act of traveling to places associated with death, disaster, or the macabre. The interest in Chernobyl has surged in recent years, fueled by documentaries, films, and the popular HBO miniseries *Chernobyl* (2019). For many, visiting Chernobyl is a way to confront the horrific reality of the disaster, to witness firsthand the aftermath of a nuclear catastrophe that altered the course of history. Tourists venture into the Exclusion Zone with guided tours, some eager to witness the decaying remnants of Pripyat, others intrigued by the idea of stepping into a world that feels like it's been frozen in time.

However, the rise in tourism has raised ethical and environmental concerns. The area is still contaminated with radioactive material, and while some parts of the Exclusion Zone have relatively low levels of radiation, others remain dangerously hazardous. The tourism industry surrounding Chernobyl has grown rapidly, with numerous companies offering day trips and longer excursions. The increased number of visitors has led to concerns about the potential spread of radiation as tourists leave the area, carrying radioactive particles on their clothing and belongings. Though tour operators take precautions, the possibility of contamination remains a serious risk.

Moreover, there is an ongoing debate about the morality of dark tourism in places like Chernobyl. For many survivors and relatives of those affected by the disaster, the sight of tourists taking selfies in front of the wreckage of Pripyat's amusement park or exploring the ruined homes of evacuees is a painful reminder of the human cost of the disaster. The commercialization of such a tragic event raises questions about the respect and sensitivity due to the victims and their families. Can the memory of such a catastrophe be appropriately preserved in a way that honors those affected, or does tourism risk reducing it to a morbid spectacle?

Despite these concerns, the lure of Chernobyl remains undeniable. Its desolate beauty, the stark contrast between man-made devastation and nature's reclamation, and the lingering sense of tragedy that permeates the area continue to captivate the imagination of those who visit. Chernobyl is, in a sense, a living monument to the dangers of unchecked technological ambition, a reminder of how human error and negligence can leave a lasting, irreversible mark on the world. As the years pass, the Exclusion Zone remains an inescapable part of our history, and its haunting ruins serve as a chilling testament to the fragility of life and the devastating power of nuclear energy.

The legacy of Chernobyl is one of both tragedy and survival. While the area remains a toxic wasteland for humans, it has become a symbol of resilience, of nature's ability to adapt and survive in the face of destruction. The plants and animals that now inhabit the Exclusion Zone continue to thrive in a land once considered too dangerous for life to exist. In a way, the creatures that now roam the abandoned streets of Pripyat are a testament to the enduring power of life, even in the most hostile of environments.

The story of Chernobyl is far from over, and as time passes, the Exclusion Zone will continue to evolve, a place where history, tragedy, and the passage of time converge. It remains a place of mystery, of mourning, and of reflection, and it is sure to captivate future generations as they seek to understand the true cost of one of history's most devastating disasters.

Chapter 8: Antarctica's Perils

Antarctica, often referred to as the Earth's final frontier, is the harshest, coldest, and driest continent on the planet. Stretching across the southernmost reaches of the Earth, it is a land of extreme contrasts, a place where life seems to exist only in the most resilient forms. The continent is enveloped in ice, and its vast expanse—nearly twice the size of Australia—covers an astonishing 14 million square kilometers. Beneath its frozen surface lies an environment that is both alien and hostile to human life. Yet, despite its forbidding nature, Antarctica continues to captivate explorers, scientists, and adventurers, driven by a relentless desire to uncover its secrets.

The extreme conditions of Antarctica are, in many ways, its most defining feature. Temperatures here can plunge to nearly -90°C (-130°F) in the winter months, with the average winter temperature hovering around -50°C (-58°F). During summer, the temperature barely rises above -20°C (-4°F) near the coast, and the continent's interior remains frigid. The winds, too, are relentless, often reaching speeds of up to 200 kilometers per hour (124 mph), further intensifying the already lethal cold. The combination of low temperatures, icy winds, and an inhospitable environment makes Antarctica one of the most dangerous places on Earth.

Yet, despite these extreme conditions, Antarctica has attracted researchers, scientists, and adventurers for decades. Its allure lies not only in its physical isolation but also in the immense scientific value that the continent holds. Beneath the thick ice sheet, which holds around 60% of the world's fresh water, there are mysteries waiting to be unlocked. Scientists have discovered evidence of ancient lakes, buried deep beneath the ice, and these bodies of water could hold clues about life forms that may have existed millions of years ago. In addition, the ice cores drilled from the continent's glaciers contain records of Earth's climate history, offering a unique window into past environments and the planet's evolution.

However, despite its promise of discovery, Antarctica's perils are vast and varied. The continent's isolation means that any exploration or research is fraught with significant challenges. The first and most immediate danger is the cold, which can cause frostbite or hypothermia within minutes of exposure. The risk of freezing limbs and losing fingers, toes, or even entire limbs to the extreme cold is a constant concern for those who venture onto the continent. To survive, researchers and adventurers must wear specialized clothing and equipment designed to protect against the freezing temperatures, including layers of thermal insulation, heated gloves, and goggles to shield their eyes from the sun's reflection off the snow.

Yet the cold is not the only danger that Antarctica poses. The continent is also home to hidden dangers that make navigating the frozen wilderness treacherous. Crevasses, deep fissures in the ice, are perhaps one of the greatest hazards. These crevasses can be as deep as 60 meters (197 feet) and span several meters wide. Often covered by a thin crust of snow, they can be nearly invisible to the unsuspecting traveler. The consequences of falling into one of these crevasses can be fatal, as rescuing a person from such a depth is incredibly difficult, if not impossible, in the harsh conditions.

Whiteouts, a phenomenon where the ground and sky become indistinguishable due to heavy snow and overcast skies, present another serious risk. In a whiteout, visibility can drop to near zero, disorienting even the most experienced explorers and leaving them vulnerable to losing their bearings and becoming lost in the vast, empty expanse. In these conditions, finding shelter or a safe path forward can be next to impossible, and getting lost in Antarctica, where the landscape is almost entirely uniform, could result in a slow, agonizing death from exposure.

Ice storms are another dangerous aspect of life in Antarctica. These storms can strike without warning, bringing high winds, freezing rain, and snow that can reduce visibility to just a few meters. In such storms, getting caught outside without proper shelter or equipment can be deadly. The winds that accompany these storms can strip away skin, damage equipment, and cause severe frostbite in a matter of minutes. Even the most carefully planned expeditions can be brought to a halt by these unpredictable and unforgiving weather patterns.

Despite these dangers, Antarctica remains an essential location for scientific research. The continent's extreme conditions provide a natural laboratory for studying climate change, glaciology, and the biology of extremophiles—organisms that thrive in the most inhospitable environments. Researchers study the ice cores drilled from the Antarctic glaciers, which provide invaluable records of Earth's climate history. These ice cores, some of which are over 800,000 years old, contain trapped bubbles of air that reveal the concentrations of greenhouse gases throughout history, helping scientists better understand the causes and effects of climate change.

In addition to its climate and environmental significance, Antarctica is also a site of ongoing exploration into life forms that may exist beneath its icy surface. Lake Vostok, located nearly 4 kilometers (2.5 miles) below the ice, is one of the largest subglacial lakes on Earth. For years, scientists have been eager to uncover what lies within this isolated environment, which has remained untouched for millions of years. Microbial life, potentially unique to the extreme conditions of the lake, could hold the key to understanding how life can survive in the most extreme environments on Earth—or even on other planets. The discovery of such life would be groundbreaking, revolutionizing our understanding of biology and the potential for life beyond Earth.

Despite the promise of these scientific breakthroughs, Antarctica's remote and perilous environment means that exploration is fraught with danger. Even with the most advanced technology, researchers must navigate treacherous conditions, constantly battling the freezing temperatures, brutal winds, and hazardous terrain. For those who venture to the continent, survival requires not only physical endurance but also mental resilience, as the psychological toll of isolation and extreme conditions can be just as deadly as the physical dangers.

In recent years, there has been growing interest in the exploration of Antarctica, driven in part by the desire to better understand climate change, as well as the mysteries hidden beneath its ice sheets. However, the increasing human presence on the continent raises concerns about the potential impact on its fragile ecosystem. Antarctica is governed by the Antarctic Treaty, an international agreement that ensures the continent is used solely for peaceful purposes and scientific research.

The treaty also imposes strict regulations on tourism and human activity to protect the environment from exploitation. However, the pressures of research and the growing interest in the continent's resources pose significant challenges to maintaining the delicate balance between exploration and preservation.

Despite its inherent dangers, Antarctica continues to captivate those who seek to uncover its secrets. It remains a place of great mystery, where the harsh conditions and untapped potential of the land create a unique environment that both challenges and inspires. From its hidden crevasses and violent storms to the scientific discoveries waiting beneath the ice, Antarctica stands as a reminder of the raw power and beauty of nature. It is a place that pushes the limits of human endurance and curiosity, a continent that remains as enigmatic and perilous as ever.

Chapter 9: Lake Natron

Lake Natron, nestled in the arid northern region of Tanzania, is a place of unsettling beauty and terrifying danger. The lake, with its eerily red waters and alkaline pH, appears to be a caustic wonderland—a place where few can survive, yet a select few creatures manage to thrive. It is a land of stark contrasts, where the stunning colors and serene landscapes belie the deadly nature of the environment. Lake Natron, a shallow, saline, and soda lake, stretches across about 1,040 square kilometers, fed primarily by the surrounding hot springs and the waters of the Ewaso Ng'iro River. Its location, bordered by the jagged peaks of the Eastern Rift Valley and nestled near the base of the active Ol Doinyo Lengai volcano, adds to the sense of isolation that permeates the area.

The water's high salinity, combined with its extreme alkalinity, makes the lake a toxic brew. With a pH level that can reach 10.5, the water is caustic enough to burn human skin upon contact. The lake's environment is inhospitable to most forms of life, yet it is home to a number of unique organisms that have adapted to the hostile conditions. The lake's red hue comes from the presence of various microorganisms, including algae and bacteria that thrive in the high salinity and alkalinity. These organisms contribute to the lake's eerie, almost otherworldly appearance, a reminder of nature's ability to adapt to extreme conditions.

Yet, the lake's dangerous waters are not the only reason Lake Natron has earned its place on the list of the world's most mysterious and dangerous places. The unique combination of environmental factors in this remote location results in a phenomenon that is both fascinating and macabre: the natural mummification of animal carcasses. The extreme conditions of the lake, including the high temperatures, mineral-rich waters, and alkalinity, preserve the bodies of animals that come into contact with the lake or its shores. For the unfortunate creatures that venture too close to the water, the toxic environment acts like a natural preservative, rendering them into haunting, calcified statues.

The process of mummification begins when an animal, often a bird, reptile, or mammal, becomes exposed to the lake's waters. The alkaline water is so harsh that it dissolves the soft tissues of the animal, while the minerals and salts in the lake's composition slowly replace the body's fluids. The result is a grotesque, frozen-in-time specimen, often calcified or encrusted with salt crystals, resembling a lifeless figure caught in an instant of time. The animals that meet this grim fate typically appear in lifelike poses, with their wings spread out or their limbs frozen in a desperate attempt to flee the fatal waters. For many, these preserved animals serve as a haunting reminder of the lake's lethal power, giving the region a sense of macabre intrigue.

In one of the most unsettling and iconic features of Lake Natron, the animals that have been mummified often retain a remarkable level of detail. The calcification process preserves the animal's outer appearance with stunning accuracy, sometimes even capturing the reflection of the surrounding landscape in their eyes. In the case of birds, particularly the hundreds of flamingos that flock to the lake's edges, the result is a striking, almost surreal visual: a collection of perfectly preserved, skeletal remains that seem to stand as a ghostly memorial to those who did not survive the lake's toxic embrace. The dead flamingos, caught in their final moments of life, are often found still clinging to their instinctive behavior, their wings frozen mid-flap or their bodies contorted in flight. For those who visit the area, it is a poignant yet chilling sight—an eerie juxtaposition of life and death, nature's cruelty and beauty.

Despite its deadly nature, Lake Natron is not entirely devoid of life. In fact, the lake is home to a unique and resilient species: the flamingo. These remarkable birds have adapted to the extreme conditions of Lake Natron, thriving in an environment that would be lethal to most other creatures. Flamingos, specifically the Lesser Flamingo, find the lake's caustic waters ideal for breeding. The high alkaline levels of the water prevent the growth of predatory fish and create a safe haven for the flamingos to lay their eggs. The lake's salt crusts provide a nesting ground for these birds, while the abundance of algae in the water supplies the flamingos' primary food source.

Flamingos are drawn to Lake Natron because the high levels of salt and algae in the water create an ideal feeding environment for them. These birds feed primarily on the algae and microorganisms that thrive in the lake's warm, mineral-rich waters. The algae contain carotenoids, the pigments that give the flamingos their signature pink color. Flamingos' bodies are able to process these carotenoids, which are then stored in their feathers, creating the vibrant hue that makes them so easily recognizable. The lake's unique combination of minerals and nutrients allows flamingos to flourish here, despite the extreme conditions that would prove fatal to other species.

However, the flamingos' relationship with Lake Natron is not without risks. Every year, thousands of flamingos migrate to the lake to breed, and many make the perilous journey across the lake's treacherous waters. While the flamingos are adapted to the environment, the lake's high temperatures and toxic waters still pose a threat. The birds must navigate the perilous conditions, carefully avoiding the shores where the alkali waters can quickly damage their delicate feathers or skin. The harsh landscape is also home to a number of natural hazards, including the volcanic activity of the nearby Ol Doinyo Lengai volcano, which can occasionally send ash and toxic fumes into the air, further adding to the dangers the birds must face.

Lake Natron's incredible survival story is also a testament to the resilience of life in extreme environments. The flamingos are not the only creatures that call this toxic place home. Along with the algae and microorganisms that sustain the flamingos, the lake is also home to a variety of bacteria and salt-loving organisms known as extremophiles. These organisms are capable of surviving in the extreme conditions of the lake, including its scorching heat, high alkalinity, and lack of oxygen. For scientists, Lake Natron offers a fascinating glimpse into the adaptability of life and the ability of organisms to thrive in some of the harshest conditions on Earth.

Despite its life-giving properties for these organisms, Lake Natron remains one of the most perilous places on Earth. The mummified remains of animals that are scattered across the shores of the lake serve as a grim reminder of the lake's danger, and the high levels of alkalinity and salt make it a near-impossible environment for human survival. Even the most prepared and cautious adventurers are at risk, with the potential for severe burns or death if they come into contact with the water. The lake's toxic nature also makes it impossible for humans to harvest its resources, making the region largely inaccessible to those who might otherwise seek to exploit its minerals.

Lake Natron remains one of the most enigmatic and fascinating places on Earth. It is a place where life and death are inextricably linked, where the forces of nature work together to preserve the past while creating an environment that continues to baffle scientists and explorers. In its otherworldly beauty and lethal toxicity, the lake serves as a reminder of the power of the natural world to shape life, death, and everything in between.

Chapter 10: The Devil's Sea

The Devil's Sea, often referred to as Japan's Bermuda Triangle, is a stretch of water located in the Pacific Ocean, off the coast of Japan, known for its mysterious reputation and eerie occurrences. Much like its more famous counterpart in the Atlantic Ocean, this maritime region has been linked to numerous disappearances of ships, planes, and even entire crews, fueling legends of supernatural forces at work. Despite its proximity to major shipping lanes, the Devil's Sea has a dark and foreboding aura that has earned it a reputation as one of the most enigmatic places on Earth. The stories of missing vessels and unexplained phenomena that have emerged from this area are as compelling as they are chilling, creating a sense of unease that has persisted for centuries.

The Devil's Sea lies off the eastern coast of Japan, stretching from the vicinity of the Ogasawara Islands to the coast of the Izu Peninsula. It is part of the larger Pacific Ring of Fire, an area of intense geological activity that is home to numerous volcanic eruptions and frequent earthquakes. The region has long been the subject of speculation and intrigue, with a variety of paranormal stories and theories surrounding the disappearances of vessels within its waters. Ships, aircraft, and even entire fleets have reportedly vanished without a trace while traversing the Devil's Sea, often under circumstances that defy rational explanation.

One of the most famous stories to emerge from the Devil's Sea involves the disappearance of the Japanese military vessel *Kaio Maru No. 5* in 1952. The ship was conducting routine operations in the area when it mysteriously vanished. Despite a large-scale search and rescue operation, no trace of the vessel or its crew was ever found. This incident, along with others like it, led to growing fears among sailors and locals about the possible presence of unknown forces within the region. The *Kaio Maru No. 5* incident became a central part of the Devil's Sea mythos, sparking widespread speculation about the area's connection to paranormal forces and contributing to its reputation as a place of danger and mystery.

Other similar stories have emerged throughout the years, with ships and planes disappearing without explanation. One notable incident involved the disappearance of a Japanese airliner in the 1950s, which vanished while flying over the Devil's Sea. Despite extensive efforts by authorities to locate the plane, no wreckage was ever found. These unexplained events have become part of the growing mythology surrounding the Devil's Sea, leading to comparisons with the more famous Bermuda Triangle. Both areas have been linked by similar patterns of strange disappearances, creating a shared sense of dread and fascination for those who study these inexplicable phenomena.

In both the Devil's Sea and the Bermuda Triangle, the disappearances are often accompanied by accounts of bizarre occurrences and mysterious forces at play. Sailors and pilots who have survived close encounters with these regions have reported strange weather patterns, such as sudden and violent storms, unexpected shifts in magnetic fields, and erratic compass readings. These disturbances in the environment have contributed to the sense of unease that pervades the area, with many believing that these events are indicative of some supernatural influence. The inexplicable nature of these occurrences, along with the widespread accounts of vanishing vessels, has fostered a deep sense of fear and mystery surrounding the Devil's Sea.

Despite the many stories of disappearances and paranormal encounters, scientific investigations into the Devil's Sea have largely focused on natural explanations. One such theory involves the region's unique geological features. The Devil's Sea lies within the Pacific Ring of Fire, an area known for its frequent volcanic activity and seismic events. The undersea terrain in this area is highly irregular, with deep trenches, active volcanoes, and shifting tectonic plates. These factors can contribute to unusual weather patterns, such as sudden and violent storms, as well as the formation of dangerous whirlpools and tidal waves. The intense magnetic anomalies that are often reported by survivors of disappearances may also be linked to the region's complex geological structure, with disturbances in the Earth's magnetic field potentially affecting navigational instruments.

Apart from the geological elements, researchers have suggested that methane gas emissions might be the reason behind the enigmatic disappearances in the Devil's Sea. Methane, a potent greenhouse gas, is often found in large pockets beneath the ocean floor, particularly in areas with active volcanic activity. When these gas pockets are disturbed, the methane can be released into the water, causing dangerous fluctuations in buoyancy and rendering vessels unstable. It is theorized that sudden methane gas releases in the Devil's Sea could explain some of the disappearances, as the gas could cause ships to sink rapidly or planes to crash.

Despite these scientific theories, local beliefs and folklore about the Devil's Sea continue to perpetuate the idea of supernatural forces at work. According to local legend, the Devil's Sea is home to vengeful spirits and malevolent entities that prey on those who venture too close to its waters. One popular myth speaks of a sea serpent that haunts the region, dragging ships and their crews into the depths. This mythical creature, believed to have been awakened by the turbulent forces of the ocean, is said to be the source of many of the unexplained disappearances. While there is no evidence to support the existence of such a creature, the legend remains an important part of the cultural narrative surrounding the Devil's Sea, contributing to the sense of dread and mystery that surrounds the area.

Another aspect of local belief is the notion that the Devil's Sea is cursed. According to some, the waters are cursed due to the violent and destructive forces that have shaped the region over millennia. The area is also known for its frequent volcanic eruptions and tectonic activity, which has led to the belief that the sea is somehow connected to the wrath of ancient gods. This sense of divine retribution is thought to be responsible for the disappearances of ships and planes, as well as the strange phenomena reported by survivors.

The Devil's Sea, like its more famous counterpart in the Atlantic, remains one of the most mysterious and dangerous places on Earth. Its combination of eerie disappearances, strange weather patterns, and supernatural legends has made it a source of fascination for explorers, researchers, and the general public. Whether one believes in the scientific explanations or the paranormal theories, the Devil's Sea continues to be a place of intrigue and fear, drawing people to its treacherous waters and inspiring tales of ghostly encounters and unsolved mysteries.

Despite the many scientific investigations that have sought to unravel the mystery of the Devil's Sea, the region continues to resist full understanding. It is a place where fact and folklore intertwine, where unexplained phenomena coexist with real-world dangers, and where the search for answers continues to captivate the imagination. As long as the sea remains a place of uncertainty, the legends surrounding it will persist, ensuring that the Devil's Sea remains one of the most compelling and dangerous locations in the world.

Chapter 11: Aokigahara Forest

Aokigahara Forest, often known as the "Sea of Trees," is one of the most chilling and haunting places in Japan. Nestled at the base of Mount Fuji, this dense forest has gained an international reputation for being a site of tragedy and sorrow. For centuries, the forest has been shrouded in an eerie sense of mystery and death. Its vast expanse of trees, twisting and intertwining in a seemingly endless labyrinth, has become infamous for the number of people who have chosen it as the final place of their lives. Known as Japan's "suicide forest," Aokigahara is not only a place of natural beauty but also one deeply tied to the nation's cultural views on death and the afterlife. Its dark reputation is both captivating and unsettling, drawing visitors, researchers, and those in search of solace to its haunting depths.

The forest's association with death can be traced back to several historical and cultural influences. In Japan, the act of taking one's own life has a complex and nuanced place within the nation's cultural history. The forest's ties to death are rooted in the long-standing belief in the spiritual world and the notion of ancestral spirits. Historically, it was believed that Mount Fuji, looming over Aokigahara, held powerful spiritual significance. The mountain itself is a sacred symbol in Japanese culture, revered by many as a place where the boundary between life and death is thin. Aokigahara, lying at its foot, has long been seen as a realm where the spirit world and the physical world converge. It is in this sacred space that countless individuals have sought to end their suffering, choosing to walk into the depths of the forest, never to return.

The forest's reputation as a place where people take their lives is not a recent phenomenon. Historical accounts dating back to the 19th century suggest that Aokigahara had a long history as a site for "ubasute," an ancient practice where elderly family members were abandoned in remote areas to die. In a culture where duty to one's family and the burden of aging were heavy, some families would leave their loved ones in the forest to pass away, believing it was a compassionate and honorable way to deal with the old and infirm. The forest, with its dense vegetation and isolation, became a place where death was not only inevitable but accepted.

However, it was in the 1950s that Aokigahara gained its most notorious reputation. The publication of a book in 1960 titled

The Complete Manual of Suicide highlighted the forest as a place to end one's life, and the book contributed to the growing association between Aokigahara and suicide. Over the decades, the forest became a known destination for those struggling with mental health, depression, and despair, seeking a quiet and final place to escape the pain of their lives. The number of suicides that have occurred in Aokigahara continues to rise, further entrenching the forest in the public's imagination as a tragic and sorrowful site.

Visitors to the forest often report an overwhelming sense of stillness upon entering the dense woods. The sound of wind and animal life seems muted by the thick canopy of trees, creating an almost unnerving silence. The atmosphere within Aokigahara is heavy, and it is easy to see why so many have described it as having an otherworldly presence. The trees are tightly packed together, blocking out the sun and creating an impenetrable darkness that adds to the foreboding mood of the place. The absence of clear paths and the winding, labyrinthine nature of the forest make it easy to become disoriented, adding to the feeling of being lost in a place that is both physically and emotionally isolating.

Local legends and folklore surrounding the forest deepen its mysterious allure. One of the most enduring tales is that of the Yurei, or restless spirits, which are said to haunt the forest. These spirits are believed to be the souls of those who have taken their own lives in the forest, unable to find peace in the afterlife. According to some, the souls of these individuals wander the woods, their spirits trapped by the darkness and isolation of the forest, unable to move on. The haunting presence of the Yurei is often described as palpable, with many visitors reporting a sensation of being watched or followed as they walk through the trees. The belief in these spirits contributes to the sense of dread that hangs over the forest, making it a place where the living and the dead seem to coexist in uneasy harmony.

Despite its grim history, Aokigahara is not without its efforts to preserve both the forest itself and the lives of those who come to it. In recent years, local authorities and mental health organizations have made concerted efforts to curb the rising suicide rates in the forest and to protect visitors from harm. Signs have been posted along the paths in the forest, urging people to reconsider their decision and offering phone numbers for suicide prevention hotlines and support services. These signs serve as a reminder that there is always hope and help available, no matter how dark the situation may seem. The initiative has been part of a larger campaign to address the mental health crisis in Japan, where issues like suicide remain a taboo subject and mental health support is often underutilized.

In addition to these efforts, there are strict regulations in place to prevent individuals from wandering too far into the forest. Search teams, consisting of local volunteers and police officers, are dispatched regularly to search the forest for signs of distress or individuals in need of assistance. This ongoing monitoring aims to reduce the number of deaths within Aokigahara and to offer support to those who may be struggling with mental health issues. These interventions, while not always successful in preventing every tragedy, show a growing recognition of the need to address the complex issues surrounding suicide and mental health in Japan.

Despite the somber and tragic history of Aokigahara, the forest is not only a place of sorrow. It is also a place of remarkable natural beauty, with a rich diversity of flora and fauna that thrives in the dense forest environment. The area is home to a number of rare species of plants and animals, and it is a popular spot for hikers and nature enthusiasts who seek to explore the forest's mysteries without delving into its darker associations. Aokigahara's volcanic soil, rich in minerals, provides a fertile ground for plant life, and the lush greenery offers a stark contrast to the darker connotations of the forest. In fact, Aokigahara is often recognized for its biodiversity and its ecological importance as a preserved forest in an otherwise developed region.

The forest's connection to Mount Fuji further enhances its significance. Mount Fuji, considered one of Japan's most sacred mountains, has long been associated with spiritual and religious practices. Pilgrims often trek to the summit, and many consider the mountain a symbol of life, death, and rebirth. Aokigahara, lying in the shadow of this sacred mountain, adds another layer of complexity to its cultural significance. It is said that the forest, in some sense, represents the natural boundary between life and death, where those who seek to end their suffering can find solitude, but also where life continues to thrive in unexpected ways.

Despite its haunting reputation, Aokigahara Forest remains an important part of Japan's cultural and natural landscape. The juxtaposition of beauty and tragedy, life and death, makes it a place that evokes both deep reverence and fear. Visitors continue to be drawn to its depths, whether out of curiosity, reverence, or a desire to experience the silence and solitude of the forest. The forest's legacy is marked by both sorrow and hope, as it continues to serve as a somber reminder of the fragility of life and the importance of mental health awareness and intervention.

In the end, Aokigahara remains one of the most perplexing and thought-provoking locations on Earth. It is a place where the human experience intersects with nature, death, and spirituality, creating a complex and multifaceted environment that continues to capture the imaginations of those who venture within. For many, Aokigahara will always be a place of darkness, but for others, it is a place of reflection, healing, and understanding. It is a testament to the complexity of life, death, and the human spirit.

Chapter 12: The Boiling River of the Amazon

The Shanay-Timpishka, also known as the "Boiling River," is one of the most extraordinary natural phenomena on Earth. Located in the depths of the Amazon rainforest in Peru, this river is unlike any other in the world. Its waters, which reach temperatures so high they are capable of scalding anything that enters, have long fascinated both scientists and indigenous people alike. Flowing through a remote part of the Peruvian jungle, the Shanay-Timpishka remains a mysterious and almost mystical place, surrounded by awe and legend. With its searing heat and mysterious origins, the river is a testament to the planet's hidden, untamed power.

The river's boiling waters are a striking sight. The temperature of the water can soar to as high as 200°F (93°C), which is far above the boiling point of water at sea level. At such extreme temperatures, the river is capable of turning nearby vegetation to mush and causing serious harm to any living creature unfortunate enough to come into contact with it. The river's scorching heat makes it impossible for most forms of life to survive in the water. Fish and other aquatic creatures are unable to withstand the high temperatures, creating a barren environment devoid of typical riverine life. The only animals that seem to thrive around the river's edges are those that have adapted to the harsh conditions, such as certain species of amphibians that can tolerate warmer waters.

For centuries, the indigenous people who live near the Shanay-Timpishka have known of the river's dangers and its significance. The indigenous tribes, such as the Mayoruna and the Matsés, have passed down stories and myths about the river's origins. According to their oral traditions, the river was created by the gods as a punishment or a blessing, depending on the tribe's interpretation of the myth. One legend speaks of a mighty serpent that once lived in the river and would boil the water with its heat to punish humans who disrespected the natural world. The serpent was eventually slain by a group of warriors, but its fiery breath forever altered the river, leaving it with its boiling properties. To the indigenous peoples, the river is not just a natural wonder but a sacred and spiritual place, holding power and meaning beyond its physical reality.

In these tribal cultures, the river is considered both a source of danger and a symbol of natural balance. The heat of the river is seen as a reflection of the balance between life and death. While the river's boiling waters are dangerous and deadly, they are also a vital part of the local ecosystem and the spiritual worldview of the indigenous people. The river's heat is tied to the power of the Earth and the supernatural forces that govern the land. To them, it is a reminder of nature's unpredictable and often unforgiving nature.

The scientific community, however, has long been baffled by the origin of the Shanay-Timpishka and its extreme temperatures. The boiling river is not located near any active volcanoes or geothermal vents, which are typically the sources of hot springs and heated rivers. The heat of the river is instead the result of geothermal activity deep below the Earth's surface, specifically the presence of a subterranean fault line that sends hot water from the Earth's interior to the surface. This unique geothermal phenomenon is what gives the river its boiling qualities.

In 2011, a team of scientists led by Andrés R. P. Ayala and a group of researchers from the Universidad Nacional Mayor de San Marcos in Lima, Peru, conducted an investigation into the river's geothermal activity. Their research revealed that the water in the river is heated by the geothermal gradient of the

Earth's crust. As the Earth's plates shift and move, magma from the planet's interior rises toward the surface, creating pockets of superheated water. The presence of hot springs in the area, combined with the geothermal fault line, allows the water in the Shanay-Timpishka to reach temperatures so high that it resembles a boiling cauldron.

Unlike typical rivers, which are fed by rainwater and runoff from higher altitudes, the Shanay-Timpishka's water is continuously replenished by the geothermal heat beneath the Earth's surface. This steady influx of heat keeps the river at its high temperatures, even in the rainy season when other rivers may swell with fresh water. The geothermal activity, while it has been studied, is still not entirely understood. Scientists are intrigued by the unique conditions that allow this phenomenon to persist and are continually exploring ways to better understand the river's geology and the forces that govern it.

The river's boiling properties have intrigued scientists, but they have also posed serious challenges for those attempting to study it. The extreme temperatures of the river make it impossible for researchers to get close to the water without risking injury or death. Previous attempts to examine the river up close have been limited to aerial surveys and remote sensing technologies. To understand the full scope of the river's geothermal activity, scientists have employed drones, thermal imaging, and other innovative methods to gather data from a safe distance. In addition to studying the river's heat, scientists have also been investigating the surrounding environment to understand how such extreme conditions impact the nearby rainforest.

One of the most fascinating aspects of the river is its role in the local ecosystem. While most animals cannot survive the intense heat of the river itself, the surrounding jungle is teeming with life. The vegetation in the area is rich and diverse, despite the high temperatures of the river. The heat from the river creates a unique microclimate that affects the plant life around it, causing certain species to thrive in the steamy, humid conditions. The nearby flora and fauna have adapted to this environment, developing specific traits that allow them to withstand the extreme conditions and flourish in the rainforest's moist, tropical atmosphere.

The Shanay-Timpishka River is a place of great wonder and danger, a living example of the Earth's incredible power and the forces of nature that we still struggle to understand. It is both a natural marvel and a deeply spiritual place for the indigenous peoples who live near it. The river's boiling waters continue to captivate the imaginations of all who learn of its existence, from scientists seeking to unravel its mysteries to travelers drawn by the allure of the unknown. In many ways, the Shanay-Timpishka is a reminder of the hidden, uncharted regions of the world that continue to inspire awe, fear, and reverence. It is a place where nature's forces are on full display, and the line between myth and reality is often blurred by the untamable power of the Earth beneath.

Chapter 13: The Haunted Catacombs of Paris

Beneath the bustling streets of Paris lies a dark and eerie secret, one that has fascinated explorers, history buffs, and paranormal enthusiasts for centuries: the Catacombs of Paris. This vast underground network of tunnels and chambers is home to the skeletal remains of an estimated six million people, making it one of the largest and most macabre ossuaries in the world. What began as a solution to the city's overflowing cemeteries in the late 18th century evolved into a haunting labyrinth that continues to draw intrigue and fear.

The story of the Catacombs begins in the late 1700s when the cemeteries of Paris were becoming overcrowded, posing serious health risks to the city's residents. The most infamous of these was the Les Innocents cemetery, located in the heart of the city, where bodies were stacked so high that they became a public health nightmare. In 1785, the French government decided to move the remains from these overcrowded burial grounds to an underground site—an abandoned limestone quarry just south of the city center. This marked the beginning of what would become the Catacombs of Paris.

The Catacombs themselves are a labyrinth of tunnels that stretch for over 200 miles (320 kilometers) beneath the city. The ossuaries, located in the southern portion of the catacombs, hold the remains of millions of Parisians who died over the centuries. As workers began to move the bones into the tunnels, they carefully arranged them into intricate patterns and stacks, creating a chillingly beautiful display of human remains. The bones, mostly skulls and femurs, are stacked in artistic arrangements along the walls, forming a macabre mosaic that has captivated visitors since it was opened to the public in the 19th century.

The sheer scale of the Catacombs is staggering. It is estimated that the ossuary holds the remains of over six million people, but this number is not precise. Many of the bones were transferred during the late 18th and early 19th centuries, a time when death was frequent due to outbreaks of plague, cholera, and other diseases. The bones of the dead were treated with a mixture of respect and practicality, as the city sought to address the growing problem of overcrowded cemeteries. The remains were sorted, cleaned, and then carefully arranged in the tunnels, creating an underground cemetery like no other.

Walking through the catacombs is an eerie and surreal experience. The narrow passageways are lined with bones, and the air is damp and heavy with the scent of the earth. As you move deeper into the network of tunnels, it becomes increasingly difficult to ignore the sense of unease that settles over you. The darkness of the catacombs is broken only by the dim light of torches and the sound of your footsteps echoing off the stone walls. For those brave enough to explore the deeper sections of the catacombs, the experience becomes even more unnerving. The tunnels seem endless, and there are sections of the catacombs that have not been fully mapped or explored, adding to the mystery of the site.

The catacombs are not just a site of historical and architectural interest, however. Over the years, they have become a magnet for paranormal activity. Numerous tales of ghostly encounters and unexplained phenomena have been reported by those who have ventured into the depths of the catacombs. Visitors have reported hearing whispers in the dark, feeling sudden cold spots, and even encountering ghostly apparitions. Some have claimed to see shadowy figures moving through the tunnels, while others have experienced the sensation of being watched. These eerie encounters have only added to the catacombs' reputation as a haunted site.

Perhaps the most famous ghost story associated with the Catacombs of Paris is the tale of the "Phantom of the Catacombs," a mysterious figure said to haunt the tunnels. According to legend, the ghost is the spirit of a long-dead Parisian who was mistakenly buried in the catacombs and now wanders the tunnels seeking revenge on those who dare to disturb his final resting place. Visitors who claim to have encountered the ghost describe a figure cloaked in tattered rags, with glowing eyes and a chilling presence. While this tale is likely a product of imagination, it adds an extra layer of mystique to the already ominous atmosphere of the catacombs.

Explorers, too, have had their share of strange experiences in the catacombs. Some have become disoriented and lost in the maze of tunnels, unable to find their way out. There are accounts of people who ventured into the catacombs and never returned, their bodies never found. While it is unclear how many of these stories are based on fact and how many have been embellished over time, the catacombs' labyrinthine structure and dark history make it an easy place for someone to vanish without a trace. In fact, a few areas of the catacombs are off-limits to the public, with the Paris police department even warning visitors about the dangers of venturing too deep into the underground system.

Despite the eerie legends and ghost stories, the Catacombs of Paris hold significant historical and cultural value. They serve as a testament to the city's long and tumultuous history, offering a glimpse into the lives—and deaths—of millions of Parisians who came before us. The catacombs are a symbol of the city's resilience, as they were created to address the public health crisis of the time and were later used for military and strategic purposes during periods of war. Today, they are a tourist attraction, drawing thousands of visitors each year who come to witness the dark beauty and historical significance of the site.

Efforts to preserve the catacombs have been ongoing since they were first opened to the public in the 19th century. In recent years, there have been concerns about the safety of the catacombs and the potential for damage to the structure. The tunnels are constantly shifting, and there is always the risk of cave-ins or other structural problems. As a result, the city of

Paris has put in place measures to protect both the catacombs and the people who visit them. The French government has invested in preservation efforts, including reinforcing the tunnels and implementing stricter access controls to limit the number of people who enter.

While the catacombs are often associated with death and the macabre, they also serve as a reminder of the fragility of life and the importance of remembering the past. The bones of the six million individuals who rest in the catacombs are a solemn reminder of the many lives lost throughout history, and their placement in the catacombs speaks to the city's reverence for those who came before. For those who venture into the catacombs, it is an experience unlike any other, one that mixes the thrill of exploration with the chilling reminder that death is never far behind.

The Catacombs of Paris remain an enigma, both captivating and unsettling. They offer a glimpse into the past, providing an eerie yet fascinating look at the history of one of the world's greatest cities. Whether you are drawn to the catacombs by their haunting beauty, their dark history, or the thrill of the unknown, one thing is certain: the underground ossuaries of Paris will continue to cast their spell on all who dare to enter, forever holding the secrets of the millions who lie within their walls.

Chapter 14: Mariana Trench

The Mariana Trench, the deepest and most enigmatic part of the world's oceans, remains one of the most elusive frontiers on Earth. Located in the western Pacific Ocean, it stretches over 1,550 miles (2,500 kilometers) in length, reaching a maximum known depth of approximately 36,000 feet (10,994 meters)—a depth that surpasses the height of Mount Everest by more than a mile. Its extreme depths make the trench not only a place of unimaginable darkness and pressure but also a site shrouded in mystery, with its vast expanse largely unexplored by humanity. It is a region where the forces of nature have shaped a world that is both alien and untouchable, a place that continues to awe and confound scientists and explorers alike.

The Mariana Trench's depth is so profound that if Mount Everest were placed at the bottom, its summit would still be over a mile underwater. The trench, formed by the subduction of the Pacific Plate beneath the smaller Mariana Plate, creates an oceanic environment unlike any other on the planet. The intense pressure at the bottom of the trench is more than 1,000 times the standard atmospheric pressure at sea level, a force that could crush most submarines and equipment designed for ocean exploration. With the depths of the trench so hostile and inaccessible, it remains one of the least explored and understood places on Earth, despite advancements in technology and scientific curiosity.

The trench is not just a void of water; it is a rich, albeit hidden, world of marine life and geological activity. Its depths are home to some of the most bizarre and unique creatures that have evolved to survive in the extreme conditions of the trench. These creatures have adapted to the crushing pressure, near-freezing temperatures, and the absence of sunlight, creating a world that seems to defy the very principles of life as we know it. Many of these species are found nowhere else on Earth, making them subjects of intense scientific interest. Among the most famous of these deep-sea dwellers are the giant amoeba, known as xenophyophores, which can grow to the size of a basketball and survive in such extreme conditions, and the deep-sea fish that glow with bioluminescence to attract prey in the pitch-black waters.

Along with these odd animals, the trench has hydrothermal vents, which are places where hot, mineral-rich water is released into the ocean by volcanic activity. These vents create a kind of oasis in the otherwise barren depths, supporting entire ecosystems that rely on chemicals rather than sunlight for sustenance. The discovery of these vents in the late 20th century revolutionized our understanding of life's potential to exist in environments previously thought to be inhospitable. Organisms that thrive near these vents include tube worms that can grow to be several feet long, with specialized bacteria living within them that convert the chemicals in the vent water into energy, providing a unique example of life's resilience and adaptability.

Despite these fascinating discoveries, much about the trench remains hidden. The difficulties of exploration are immense, and only a few expeditions have successfully reached the bottom of the trench. One of the most notable of these was the 2012 solo journey of filmmaker James Cameron, who piloted a submersible to the bottom of the Mariana Trench, making him the first person to do so in nearly 50 years. The pressures and darkness encountered at such depths are so extreme that they challenge the very limits of human technology and endurance. Cameron's journey was a landmark in ocean exploration, yet even his submersible was only able to explore a small section of the trench, leaving much of its mysteries still unexplored.

The challenges of exploring the trench are not only technical but also environmental. The trench's location, more than 200 miles east of the Mariana Islands, makes it a difficult site to access, and the surrounding area is subject to frequent seismic activity due to the tectonic movements that formed the trench. These movements make the environment unpredictable, further complicating efforts to study the trench's depths. Additionally, the darkness and cold temperatures of the trench make it difficult to gather meaningful data over extended periods. Even the best submersibles and robotic probes are limited in the amount of time they can spend at such depths before being crushed or running out of power.

Yet, despite these challenges, scientists are continuously working to better understand the trench and its secrets. Advances in technology, such as more durable submersibles and remotely operated vehicles (ROVs), are gradually opening up new avenues of exploration. In recent years, there have been several important scientific discoveries about the trench, including the identification of new species, geological formations, and the discovery of previously unknown life forms in the trench's depths. For example, in 2018, a Japanese research team discovered a new species of snailfish living at depths of more than 26,000 feet (7,900 meters) in the trench, a remarkable finding that further emphasizes the trench's role as a hidden and thriving ecosystem.

However, much remains to be discovered. One of the most intriguing aspects of the Mariana Trench is the fact that it is still largely unexplored. The trench is so vast and so deep that it remains one of the last frontiers of scientific discovery on Earth. Its mysterious and unexplored depths continue to captivate the imaginations of scientists, explorers, and the general public alike. The vast, dark expanse of the trench holds the potential for countless new discoveries, whether in the form of strange creatures, ancient geological formations, or clues about the origins of life on Earth.

The trench also holds significant scientific importance for understanding the dynamics of our planet's oceans. As the deepest part of the Earth's oceans, the Mariana Trench plays a critical role in the global climate system, helping to regulate ocean circulation and influence the carbon cycle. The trench's geological activity, including the subduction of the Pacific Plate, also has implications for understanding earthquakes, volcanic activity, and the movement of tectonic plates. Studying the trench can provide valuable insights into the processes that shape our planet and the forces that govern the Earth's oceans and atmosphere.

The Mariana Trench is more than just the deepest point on Earth; it is a symbol of the unknown, a place that challenges our understanding of life, nature, and the limits of human exploration. It represents the untapped potential of our planet's mysteries, a reminder of how much we have yet to discover about the world around us. As we continue to push the boundaries of exploration and technology, the Mariana Trench will undoubtedly continue to hold secrets that will shape our understanding of the Earth and the universe for years to come. The abyss remains as deep, dark, and mysterious as ever, awaiting the next wave of explorers brave enough to venture into its depths.

Chapter 15: The World's Loneliest Place

The Kerguelen Islands, often referred to as "The World's Loneliest Place," are a remote and desolate volcanic archipelago situated in the southern Indian Ocean, about 1,000 miles from the nearest landmass. Also known as the "Desolation Islands," they stand as one of the most isolated and inhospitable places on Earth. The islands are a part of France's Southern and Antarctic Lands, an overseas territory that includes other remote islands and territories scattered throughout the southern oceans. Despite their distance from the mainland, the Kerguelen Islands have a long history of scientific interest and exploration, making them a significant location in the study of Earth's natural processes.

The Kerguelen Islands consist of approximately 300 islands, with the largest being Grande Terre, which stretches for about 150 miles (240 kilometers) in length. Grande Terre, the archipelago's main island, is mountainous and jagged, with peaks that rise sharply from the surrounding sea. The islands' volcanic origins are apparent, as the landscape is marked by vast fields of lava, craggy ridges, and deep valleys. These geological features make the Kerguelen Islands a prime location for studying volcanic activity, as well as the broader processes of island formation and geological evolution. The islands are located on the Kerguelen Plateau, an underwater feature that plays a vital role in the regional oceanography of the southern Indian Ocean.

However, despite the archipelago's geological significance, the most striking aspect of the Kerguelen Islands is their extreme isolation. The harsh climate and remote location make them one of the most difficult places on Earth to access. The weather conditions on the islands are notoriously severe, with strong winds, frigid temperatures, and frequent storms that can make travel to the islands nearly impossible. During the winter months, temperatures can plummet below freezing, and the islands are often shrouded in a thick mist that further reduces visibility. Even in the summer, the weather remains unpredictable, with powerful gales and heavy rainfall that make daily life challenging for those who venture to the islands.

The combination of isolation, harsh weather, and rugged terrain creates a landscape that feels both timeless and hostile.

The Kerguelen Islands are so remote that the nearest human settlements are located thousands of miles away, and the only people who regularly visit are scientists and researchers who are stationed on the islands for extended periods of time. The islands' lack of a permanent population and the absence of a commercial economy give them an eerie, uninhabited quality. There are no permanent roads, no bustling cities, and no infrastructure beyond the minimal facilities needed to support scientific endeavors. This solitude has contributed to the islands' reputation as one of the loneliest places on Earth.

The isolation of the Kerguelen Islands has also made them a unique laboratory for scientific research. Despite their remote location, the archipelago is home to a variety of research stations, most notably the French research base, Port-aux-Français, which serves as the primary hub for scientific activity on the islands. The station is staffed year-round by scientists and support staff who conduct a wide range of studies related to ecology, geology, oceanography, and climatology. The Kerguelen Islands' isolated environment offers researchers a rare opportunity to study ecosystems and geological processes that remain largely unaffected by human activity, providing a valuable perspective on natural phenomena that can be difficult to observe in more populated regions.

The flora and fauna of the Kerguelen Islands are particularly notable for their adaptability to the harsh conditions. Despite the extreme weather and lack of vegetation, the islands support a surprising variety of life. The Kerguelen Islands are home to several species of seabirds, including the endemic Kerguelen petrel and the light-mantled sooty albatross, which are among the few creatures capable of surviving in such an unforgiving environment. There are also populations of seals, such as the Antarctic fur seal, and several species of penguins, including the King Penguin, which can be found in the archipelago's more sheltered coastal areas. The islands' ecosystems, though relatively sparse, have evolved to cope with the challenges of the environment, and their resilience makes them a focus of study for biologists interested in the adaptability of life in extreme conditions.

The harshness of the Kerguelen Islands has not deterred explorers, however. The islands have a rich history of exploration, dating back to the late 18th century. The French explorer Yves-Joseph de Kerguelen, for whom the islands are named, was the first to chart the archipelago in 1772.

Kerguelen's voyage was part of his broader mission to explore the southern regions of the world, and his discovery of the islands marked a significant moment in the history of Antarctic exploration.

Despite his initial belief that the Kerguelen Islands were a large landmass, further exploration revealed the archipelago's true size and remote nature, and it became clear that the islands were of little use for settlement or trade. Nevertheless, the Kerguelen Islands remained an important stop for explorers and navigators heading toward the Southern Ocean and Antarctica.

In the 20th century, the strategic location of the Kerguelen Islands made them a valuable asset for scientific research. During World War II, the islands were briefly used by the Allies for military purposes, though the harsh climate and isolation made long-term occupation impractical. After the war, the French government established research stations on the islands to support scientific studies in the fields of oceanography, biology, and geology. Since then, the Kerguelen Islands have remained a hub for scientific research, with scientists continuing to study everything from climate change to the impact of volcanic activity on marine ecosystems.

The extreme isolation of the Kerguelen Islands has also contributed to their mystique. Few people have had the privilege of visiting the archipelago, and fewer still have stayed for extended periods of time. For those who do make the journey, the Kerguelen Islands present a stark, haunting beauty that is unlike any other place on Earth. The isolation is both a challenge and an allure, offering an opportunity to experience a world largely untouched by modern civilization. It is a place where the forces of nature are at their most raw and powerful, and where the silence of the landscape is deafening.

Beyond the isolation, the Kerguelen Islands are also surrounded by the mystery of the unknown. Despite their relatively small size, the archipelago's rugged terrain and harsh weather have kept large portions of the islands unexplored. The challenges of accessing the islands, combined with the harsh conditions and the lack of infrastructure, make it difficult to fully understand the islands' potential. The surrounding waters are equally mysterious, with reports of strong ocean currents and unusual marine phenomena that remain poorly understood. This sense of mystery adds to the allure of the Kerguelen Islands, further solidifying their place as one of the world's most isolated and enigmatic locations.

Though the Kerguelen Islands may not offer the picturesque beauty of tropical paradises or the cultural significance of well-known landmarks, they represent an entirely different kind of appeal—a raw, untouched wilderness that challenges the limits of human endurance. For those who visit, the islands offer a unique opportunity to experience the Earth in its most primal form, a place where nature reigns supreme and human presence is a rare and fleeting occurrence. The Kerguelen Islands are not a destination for the faint of heart, but for those who seek the ultimate escape from civilization, they provide a solitude that is unmatched anywhere on Earth.

Conclusion

The allure of the unknown has captivated human beings for centuries. From the deepest oceans to remote wildernesses, humanity's fascination with places that lie beyond understanding has sparked curiosity and exploration. These locations, often dangerous or forbidden, hold an irresistible draw. They challenge our perceptions, pushing us to explore the limits of our endurance and knowledge.

But why do we feel compelled to explore the unknown? Perhaps it's the desire to conquer mystery and uncover truths that have eluded us. There's something deeply primal about standing at the edge of the impossible, confronting the world's greatest secrets. These places aren't just locations—they're symbols of human curiosity, resilience, and the pursuit of knowledge. They remind us of our unyielding drive to explore the world and face the mysteries it holds.

As we've explored the world's most perilous and enigmatic corners—from the eternal flames of the Darvaza Gas Crater to the forbidding isolation of North Sentinel Island—it's clear that our fascination extends beyond mere adventure. The most dangerous places are often those deemed inhospitable, forbidden, or inaccessible. These are places that defy our understanding, drawing us in because they represent something beyond the ordinary. They are wild, untamed, and offer glimpses into worlds that remain elusive, reminding us of how little we know.

These locations also teach us important lessons. Many of the places we've examined—the Kerguelen Islands, Snake Island, and Chernobyl—remind us of the fragility of life and our vulnerability in the face of nature's power. These places reveal how small we are in comparison to the forces shaping our world. In modern society, where we've learned to dominate much of the environment, these locations stand as humbling reminders of the unpredictable forces that remain beyond our control.

More than that, these places highlight the importance of respecting nature. The delicate ecosystems in these dangerous areas need protection. For instance, Snake Island's deadly snakes and the Kerguelen Islands' unique wildlife serve as stark examples of environments that must be treated with care. Our exploration of these locations must come with a deep respect for the ecosystems that sustain them. Too often, human interference has altered or even destroyed these natural wonders, leaving irreversible consequences. It's vital that we tread lightly in these spaces, recognizing our impact and ensuring that we don't disrupt the fragile balance.

The stories we've uncovered also remind us of the significance of history and culture. The Bermuda Triangle, Mount Everest's Death Zone, and the many myths and legends surrounding these locations are rich in history. They are shaped by human experiences, offering insights into the cultures and events that have defined them. To truly respect these places, we must appreciate their histories and the lessons they offer, learning from both the myths and the realities that come with them.

As we reflect on the explorers, scientists, and adventurers who have ventured into these dangerous areas, we understand that curiosity and respect must go hand in hand. Many of these individuals have risked everything, facing extreme danger and, in some cases, even losing their lives. Their stories serve as a reminder that these places demand respect. They are not mere curiosities to be conquered but environments that require careful navigation and an understanding of the risks they pose.

The dangerous and mysterious places we've explored in this book are not just physical locations but powerful symbols of the unknown. They challenge our knowledge, push us to our limits, and inspire us to uncover the mysteries they hold. These places serve as reminders of the power and beauty of nature, and they call us to approach them with humility and respect. To continue exploring without harm, we must be responsible stewards, preserving these unique ecosystems and histories for future generations. The lessons from these places are clear: only by respecting the natural world can we hope to unlock its deepest secrets without causing lasting harm.

Printed in Great Britain
by Amazon